EXP TORY

# The Romans in Britain

DOROTHY MORRISON

Oliver & Boyd

# Contents



# Topics for Workguides

1. Britain before the Romans
2. The Conquerors
3. Rebellion
4. Life with the Romans – at home
5. Fighting for Rome
6. Building and Travelling
7. A Roman Family
8. The Empire
9. Looking at the Evidence
10. Roman Influence


The author and publishers wish to thank the following for permission to reproduce the undernoted copyright material:

Aerofilms Limited 27; Cambridge University Collection (copyright reserved) 5, 45; City Museum, Gloucester 25; Colchester and Essex Museum 13; Controller of Her Majesty's Stationery Office (Crown copyright) 28, 30, 32 (left), 33; Ermine Street Guard (photographs of actual members of the Guard) 10, 22, 23; Faber and Faber Ltd 33 (lines from 'Roman Wall Blues' reprinted from *Collected Shorter Poems* by W. H. Auden); Grosvenor Museum, Chester 46; Landesmuseum, Trier 34; Mansell Collection ii, 18 (upper) photo: Alinari, 24, 29, 36; Museum of Antiquities, Newcastle upon Tyne 32 (right); The Museum of London 17 (lower); National Museum of Wales 6 (right); Reading Museum 17 (upper); Scarborough Museum 43; Skulpturensamlung, Dresden 18 (lower); Trustees of the British Museum 6 (left), 7, 35, 37, 39 (left), 47; Warburg Institute 39 (right).

OLIVER & BOYD
Robert Stevenson House
1–3 Baxter's Place
Leith Walk
Edinburgh EH1 3BB

*A Division of Longman Group Limited*





First published 1978
Fifth impression 1986

ISBN 0 05 003056 6

Produced by Longman Group (FE) Ltd
Printed in Hong Kong

Roman soldiers about to disembark

# Introduction

Imagine you are a Briton standing on the cliffs of Dover watching 50 strange ships approaching from Gaul [France]. You can see that the ships are full of armed soldiers. You have heard who these foreign soldiers are and you want to stop them conquering your country as they have conquered Gaul.

It is the year 55 BC. The ships are bringing the Roman general, Julius Caesar, who had conquered Gaul, to Britain. Caesar decided not to land at Dover. He wrote later

I saw the enemy forces standing under arms along the cliff tops. At this point of the coast very steep cliffs tower above the water. Therefore it was possible for the Britons to fire directly onto the beaches.

*1. Were the Britons in a good position? Explain your answer.*

The Romans had to sail further east along the coast to Walmer near Deal. Although there were no cliffs there, the Britons still had an advantage over the Romans, as Caesar explains.

The [Roman] troops who did not know the area, had a very hard task. Although they were weighed down with heavy armour they had to jump from their ships, stand firm in the surf, and fight at the same time.

On the other hand, Caesar said

The enemy [the Britons] knew their background. They could hurl their weapons boldly from dry land or shallow water and gallop their horses which were trained for this kind of work.

*1. Roman soldiers were used to fighting on land. Write down three reasons why it was hard for them to fight well on this occasion.*
*2. Do you think the Britons were wise to attack the Romans as they tried to land? Give a reason for your answer.*

Eventually the Romans won this battle but their fleet was badly damaged by a storm. Caesar went back to Gaul.

The next year, 54 BC, Caesar returned with a much bigger army. He landed peacefully on the Kent coast and then fought his way to the north of the River Thames. Finally, he made peace with the Britons and exacted tribute [taxes] from the king of the area he had conquered, but had to return to Gaul because of rebellions against the Romans there.

The Romans did not return to Britain for nearly a hundred years.

This book will show you some of the evidence or clues which help us to find out how Britain became a Roman province and what life was like for the people who lived in Roman Britain.

# 1 Britain before the Romans

When the Romans came to Britain the country was divided into a number of kingdoms and tribes.

Caesar found Britain rather like Gaul. He said:

There is an infinite number of men, and very many dwellings similar to those in Gaul, and many flocks.

Many Britons were farmers and herdsmen who lived in thatched houses like those in the picture below.

*1. (a) Write down four different jobs which the people in the picture are doing.*

*(b) Can you see the blacksmith? Write down three things he has made.*

*2. What animals can you see? How might they be used?*

*3. There is a strong fence round the house. What does this suggest?*

*4. Look at the two pictures on page 5. They show two ways in which people tried to protect themselves. Describe what they have done.*

The Romans sometimes conquered new lands to obtain metals or grain or other useful goods. They had to decide whether it would be worthwhile to conquer Britain. Strabo, a Roman writer, said Britain produced

corn, cattle, gold, silver, and iron . . . also hides, slaves and clever hunting dogs.

Caesar wrote,

Tin is found in the interior region, and iron at the coast, though in small quantities; the bronze they use is imported. There is timber of all the kinds known in Gaul, besides beech and fir.

1. *Make a list of the metals the Romans might hope to take from Britain.*
2. *List other products of Britain which would be useful to the Romans and suggest how they might use them.*
3. *The people of Gaul were related to some of the people of Southern Britain and had received help from them against the Romans. Suggest another reason why the Romans might wish to conquer Britain.*

Aerial views of Iron Age (or Celtic) forts:
(above) Maiden Castle, Dorset;
(below) Traprain Law, East Lothian

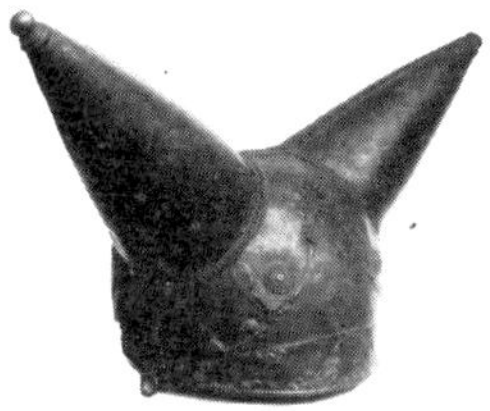

Celtic helmet, shield
(about 75 cm long),
sword (about 40 cm long),
and spearhead (about 50 cm long)

Although the Britons were farmers and herdsmen they were also fierce fighters who made fine weapons.

On the left are some of the weapons and armour made by the Britons. The shield and helmet are made of bronze.

1. *What metal might the sword and spear be made of?*

Caesar describes Britons prepared for battle.

But all the Britons stain themselves with woad, which produces a blue colour and thereby appear more frightening in battle; they wear their hair long and are clean-shaven except for their heads and upper lips.

Look at the picture on the right of a British war chariot.

1. *Do you think the chariot would be light or heavy to drive? Say why.*

Caesar says,

This is the manner of their fighting from war chariots. First they drive along throwing their spears, and by the terror caused by the horses and the noise of the wheels they generally succeed in throwing into confusion the ranks of the enemy.

1. *What three things helped to confuse their enemies in battle?*
2. *What might be particularly frightening to foot soldiers?*

Caesar says

The British horsemen were fearless and swift.

As a result of daily exercise, the swiftness of the horsemen and the steadiness of the infantry was such that they could rein in their excited horses even in very steep places, and rapidly check and turn them. They would run along the pole of the chariot and stand on the yoke, and from there rapidly run back to the chariot.

1. *Why were they able to control their horses so well?*
2. *What different actions could they perform?*

This model of a Celtic chariot
can be seen in the Welsh National Museum

# 2 The Conquerors

This Roman coin is now in the British Museum. It shows a Roman Emperor wearing the laurel wreath awarded to military leaders who have won a great victory. The Emperor's name was Claudius. In AD 43, nearly 100 years after Julius Caesar had left Britain, Claudius sent an army of over 40 000 men to conquer it. Roman emperors liked to make a name for themselves as great soldiers. After a famous victory they would be given a special triumphal procession in Rome.

Claudius, a man of 50, had only recently become emperor. The previous emperor had been murdered.

A Roman writer, Suetonius, who did not admire Claudius, tells us,

Claudius's only campaign was of no great importance. . . . He thought that Britain was the country where a real triumph could be most easily earned. . . . He marched north through Gaul, crossed the Channel without trouble and was back in Rome six months later. He had fought no battles and suffered no casualties, but made a large part of the island submit.

1. *Why did Suetonius think Claudius had decided to invade Britain?*
2. *How long did the campaign last?*
3. *How many battles did he fight?*
4. *Pick out the statements which show that Suetonius did not admire Claudius. Would his remarks be reliable or unreliable?*

Claudius sent Aulus Plautius to command his army.

His ships were ready on the coast of Gaul. However, Dio Cassius, an early writer of Roman history, tell us

He had difficulty in persuading his army to go there. For the soldiers were indignant at the thought of fighting battles outside the known world.

They nearly refused to obey his orders altogether.

1. *What earlier descriptions about Britain do you think the commander might have looked at before he set out?*
2. *The soldiers were unwilling to go to Britain. Pick out the words which show that the Romans knew very little about Britain.*

The Britons had received intelligence reports which showed that the Romans would not come, and so they had not gathered an army. Even when they did get an army together, they would not come into the open to fight the Romans, but skulked around in the swamps and the forests hoping to wear the invaders down.

*1. Why were the Romans allowed to land without a fight?*
*2. What do you think is meant by intelligence reports?*
*3. Why were the Britons unwilling to come out and face the Romans in a big battle? Do you think this was a good idea?*

The map shows where the different tribes in the south of Britain lived.

Some of the tribes were unfriendly towards each other. Tacitus, a Roman writer, says,

It is seldom that two or three states unite to fight a common danger.

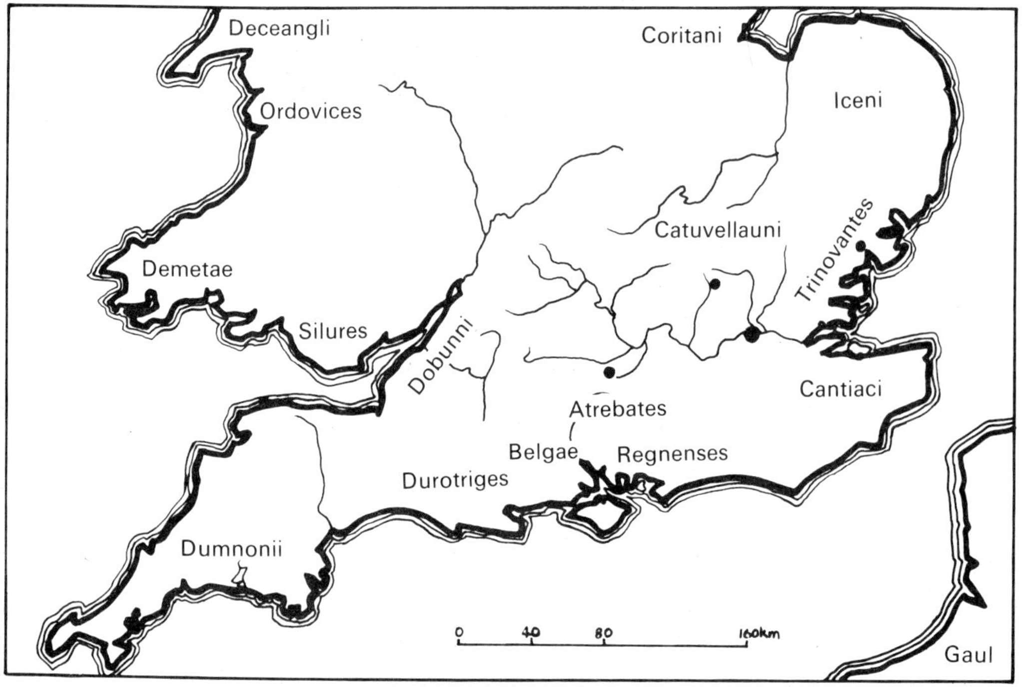


One group of tribes living in the south-east of Britain did join together. They accepted the leadership of the King of the Catuvellauni tribe. When he died they were lead by his two sons Caractacus and Togodumnus. Their warriors fought with iron spears and swords and carried shields made of leather and bronze. They wore leather armour. Like the Britons Caesar had described earlier, they were skilled charioteers. Their army was strong but less well trained and organised than the Roman troops. Once it was defeated the other tribes in the south-east did not really oppose the Romans.

*1. How would the unfriendliness of the tribes towards each other help the Romans?*
*2. Suggest why the tribes in the south-east of Britain might have joined together.*

When the Romans reached the Thames, the Emperor Claudius arrived. He stayed in Britain only sixteen days in order to receive the leaders of the conquered tribes. Then he hurried back to Rome to celebrate his great military triumph. There he had a large stone carved with this inscription in Latin:

Without any mishap he received in unconditional surrender eleven conquered British kings.

*1. Do you think Claudius deserved the triumphal procession? Say why.*

Caractacus escaped west to the mountains of Wales. He tried to get the tribes there to fight against the Romans, using the hit and run methods of guerilla warfare.

For several years Caractacus caused trouble for the Romans but in the end he was betrayed in AD 51 and taken, with his wife and daughter and other relatives, to Rome. Although he was a captive in chains, he behaved with great dignity, looking calm and unafraid as he walked along the hot Roman streets in a procession organised by Claudius to show off his prisoners. The crowd pressed forward eagerly to see him.

The Roman writer Tacitus tells us that when Caractacus was brought before the Emperor Claudius, he said

I had horses, men, arms, wealth. Are you surprised that I am sorry to lose them? If you want to rule the world, does it follow that everyone else welcomes slavery?

Claudius decided to free Caractacus and his family but he was not allowed to return to Britain.

1. *Why do you think Claudius had Caractacus brought to Rome?*
2. *What do you think Caractacus expected would happen to him?*
3. *Why do you think he was set free?*
4. *Why would he not be allowed to return home?*

Claudius's triumphal procession in Rome (artist's reconstruction)

# 3 Rebellion

Roman legionary
(Ermine Street Guard)

This woman gathered a huge army. She was very tall and terrifying with fierce eyes and a harsh voice. A great mane of red hair hung down to her hips. Round her neck was a large gold necklace. She wore a tunic of many colours, and over this was a thick cloak fastened with a brooch. She grasped a spear to help her look more terrifying.

This is how a Roman, Dio Cassius, described Boadicea.

Boadicea was queen of the Iceni tribe. The map on page 8 shows where they lived. The Iceni and other local tribes had been badly treated by some of the Roman tax-collectors. Boadicea and her daughters had been insulted and scorned when they complained.

Retired Roman soldiers had been allowed to found a colony at Camulodunum, which had once been the capital of the Catuvellauni tribe. It is now Colchester. They lived there with their wives and families. Each retired soldier was given a piece of land.

1. *Write down two things which made Boadicea seem a terrifying leader.*
2. *Who would have owned the land before the retired Roman soldiers?*
3. *Why might the local Britons feel angry towards these Romans?*

According to Dio Cassius Boadicea made a stirring speech to her troops, urging them on to attack the Romans.

You have come to realise how much better it is to be poor with no master, than to be a rich slave. We would have been better off if we had been killed rather than going about with a tax on our heads. It is our own fault we let them land in the first place instead of chasing them out at once as we did with the famous Julius Caesar.

1. *Explain in your own words what Boadicea meant by saying 'how much better it is to be poor with no master than to be a rich slave.'*
2. *What complaint did Boadicea have about Roman rule?*

The Roman army was well-trained and well-equipped. Unlike the Britons, Roman soldiers wore a uniform. Unless he was prepared for battle, the Roman soldier carried all his bedding and equipment and food on his back as he marched. (The weight was about 60 Roman pounds. One Roman lb = $327\frac{1}{2}$ gms.)

1. *Make a list of the weapons the legionary in the picture has. Which weapons would he use most?*
2. *His body armour is made in sections joined by leather cords. What advantage would this have?*
3. *Many Britons fought bare-headed. How was the Roman's head protected?*

Boadicea's followers might well have been afraid to fight against soldiers like this but according to Dio Cassius she told her people:

There are more of us and we are braver. They have protected themselves with helmets and breastplates and they put up fences and walls and trenches to make sure that no one can attack them. If they were not afraid they would come out and fight as we do. We think our tents are safer than their walls. Our shields are a better protection than their whole suits of armour. If we ever choose to retreat anywhere we hide in the swamps and mountains so that we cannot be found. But because of their heavy armour our enemies cannot chase anybody or run away.

1. *What defence did the Romans build against attack?*
2. *Boadicea claimed that the Britons were braver than the Romans. Do you think this was true? Give a reason for your answer.*

Boadicea said that the Romans could not

take hunger, thirst, cold or heat as we can. They need shade and covering. They need bread and wine and oil, and if they cannot get all these things they cannot survive.

The Britons could live much more simply.

We can use grass or roots as bread, the juice of any plant as oil, any water as wine, any tree as a house.

Finally

We know the land. They don't.

1. *Why might Boadicea believe the Romans could not survive if they could not get certain supplies?*
2. *How would the fact that they could live more simply help the Britons?*

## Destruction at Colchester

Within a few days Boadicea and her followers attacked the colony of retired soldiers at Camulodunum [Colchester]. There were no walls round the town so the Romans all took refuge in the biggest building. This was the Temple of Claudius.

The picture below shows what the temple may have looked like.

1. *Why would the Britons attack Colchester first?*
2. *(a) Why would the Romans try to shelter in the temple of Claudius?*
   *(b) The Britons set the roof of the temple on fire. Would the Romans find it easy to escape?*

Temple of Claudius at Colchester (artist's reconstruction)

## The Revolt Spreads

The map below shows the Roman towns which the Britons attacked. They destroyed Colchester and killed all the Romans they could find. Then they moved south to Londinium which did not have a town wall.

*1. What might the people of Londinium do when they heard what had happened at Colchester?*

All the people who remained in Londinium were killed by the Britons with great cruelty. The Britons moved on to Verulamium. They destroyed and killed all the people they found there. A Roman writer tells us many thousands of people were killed, probably just about all the men, women and children who were in the three towns at the time.

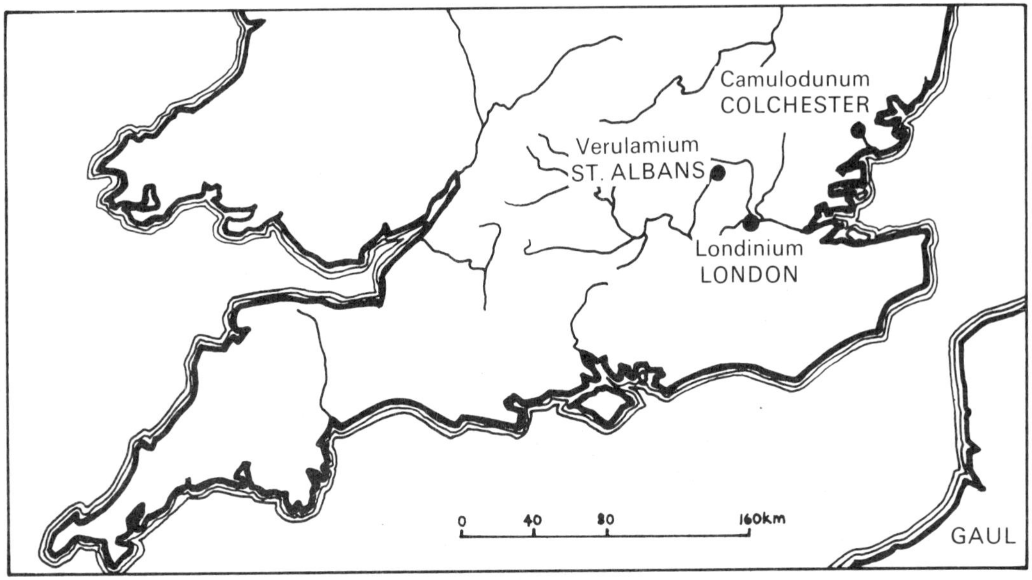


The picture on page 13 shows the tombstone of a Roman soldier from the cemetery at Colchester. It dates from the time of the Emperor Claudius. The stone was found broken in half. At one time long ago someone has deliberately damaged the face by breaking off the nose, perhaps to show contempt for the Romans.

*1. Suggest a way in which the tombstone might have been damaged.*

The Britons were greatly encouraged by their successes. Boadicea urged them on to fight again. Tacitus tells us,

> Boadicea drove round all the tribes in a chariot with her daughters in front of her. 'We British are used to women commanders in war,' she cried. 'I am descended from mighty men! But I am not fighting for my kingdom and wealth now. I am fighting as an ordinary person for my lost freedom, my beaten body, and my ill-treated daughters. The Roman division which dared to fight is wiped out! The others cower in their camps or watch for a chance to escape. They will never face even the din and roar of all our thousands.'

*1. Was it usual or unusual for a woman to lead an army of Britons?*

*2. Why do you think the Britons were ready to follow Boadicea?*

*3. Did Boadicea think the Britons would defeat the Romans? Say why.*

One reason why the Britons were able to do so much damage was that the main part of the Roman army was elsewhere in Wales. When the Roman army hurried back across to the south-east and met up with the Britons there was a fierce battle which the Romans eventually won. After her successes this was a bitter blow to Boadicea. She was the proud queen of a great tribe. Unable to face the disgrace and humiliation of becoming a Roman prisoner she drank poison and died.

The Roman soldiers killed or punished many Britons but the Emperor sent a new military commander. He stopped the punishment. Better officials were sent to govern the Britons and to try to establish the Roman way of life more peacefully.

*1. How might Boadicea have been treated by the Romans? (Remember Caractacus.)*

*2. Do you think the Britons were right to rebel in this way? Why?*

*3. Why do you think the government in Rome decided to stop punishing the Britons? Was this wise?*

Part of the tombstone of M. Favonius Facilis, Centurion

# 4 Life with the Romans~ at home

The picture below is of the centre of Rome as it was about the third century AD. As you can see, it is a city of fine buildings with graceful pillars and statues, theatres, temples, public baths and open squares.

When the Romans came to Britain they brought their ideas and way of life with them. They built houses in the Roman style and richer Britons copied these designs. New towns grew up in Britain with buildings like those in Rome.

Valerius was a rich British merchant who lived with his family in the Roman town of Calleva Atrebatum [Silchester].

Look at the pictures of this town on page 15.

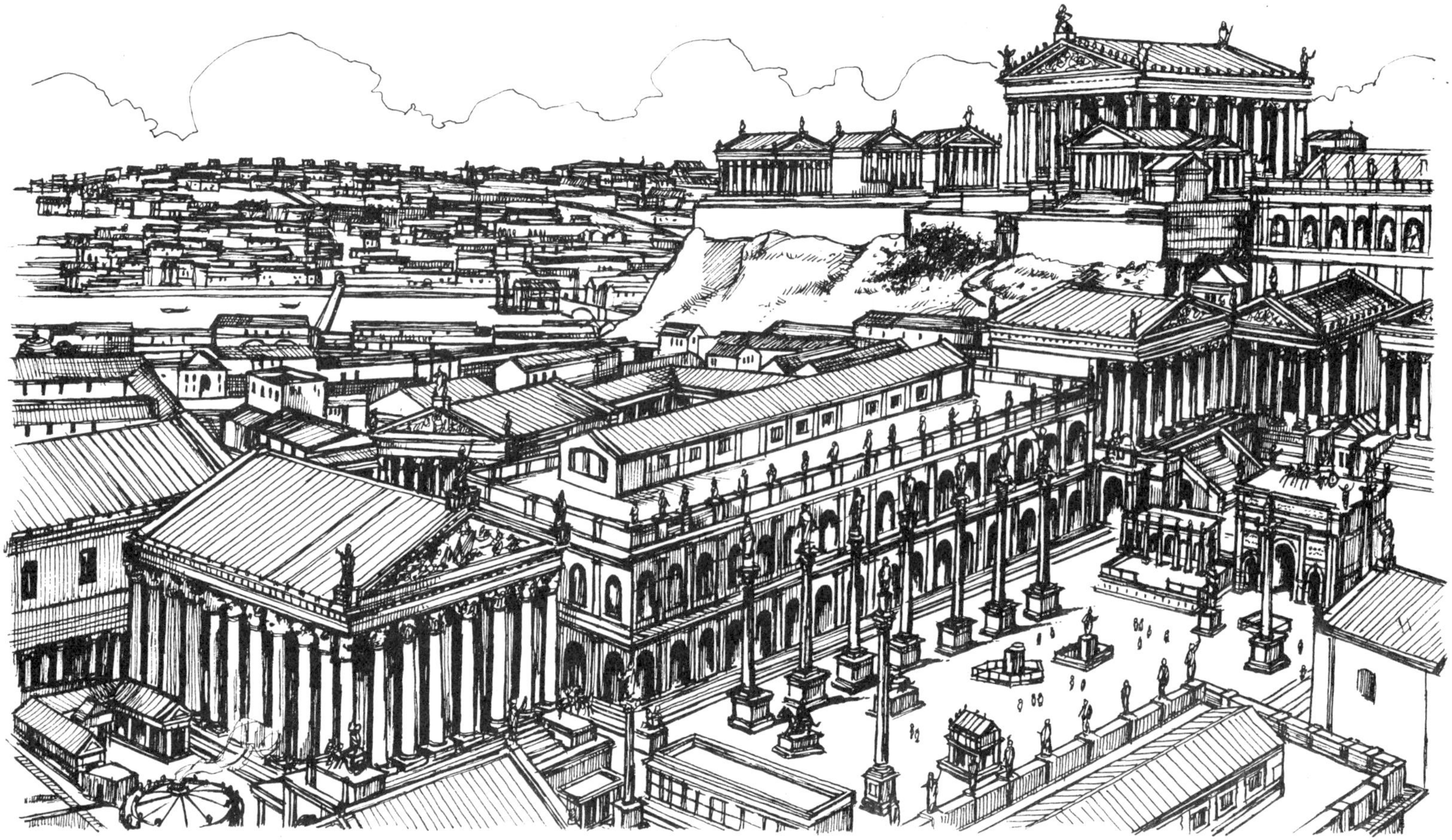

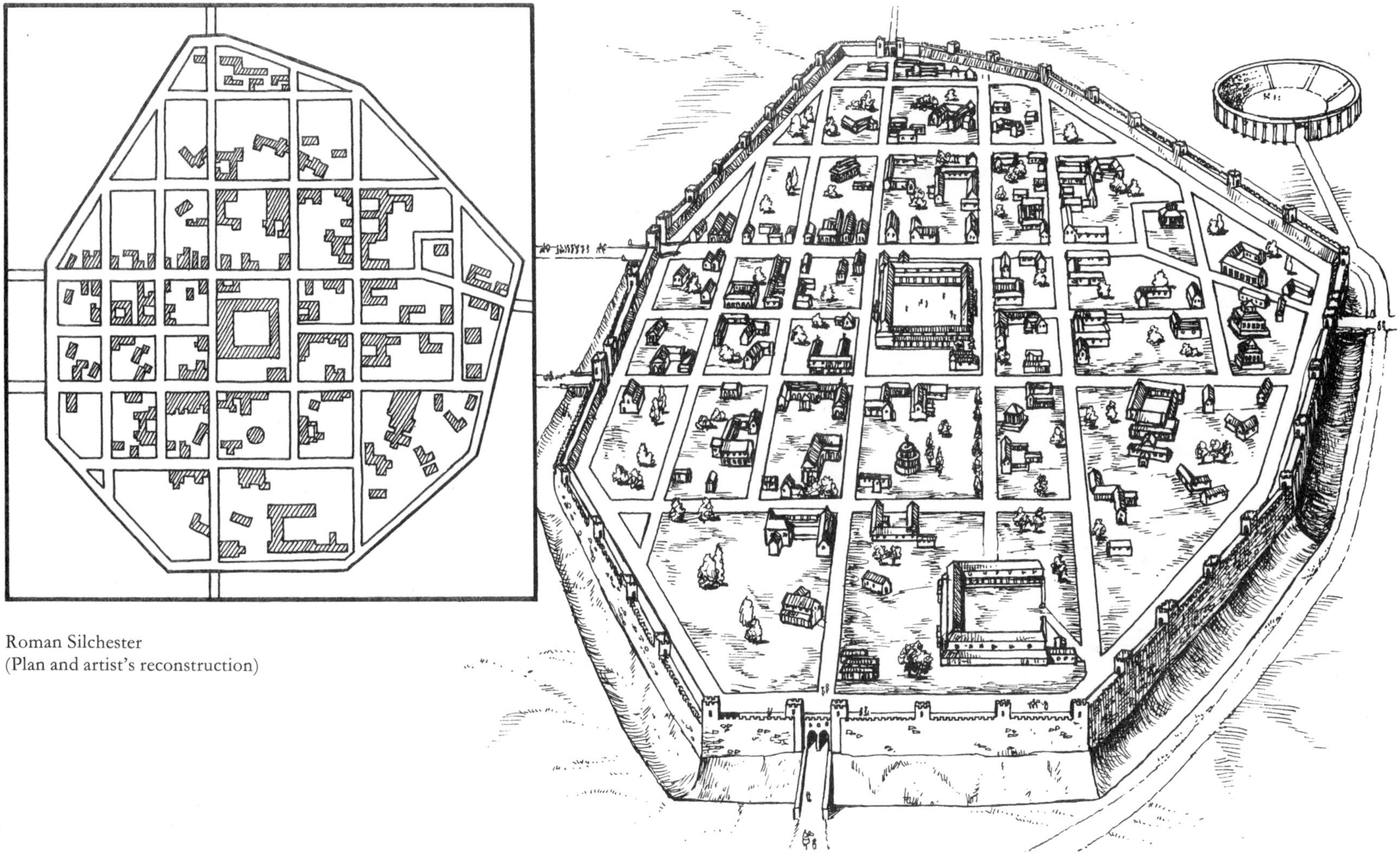

Roman Silchester
(Plan and artist's reconstruction)

*1. Examine the way the streets are laid out. From the list below choose the words which you think best describe the streets' layout.*

| | |
|---|---|
| *Winding* | *Well-arranged* |
| *Straight* | *Neat* |
| *Irregular* | *Confused* |

Valerius often met with other merchants to do business at the basilica or town hall. It was in the forum and was the most important building in the town.

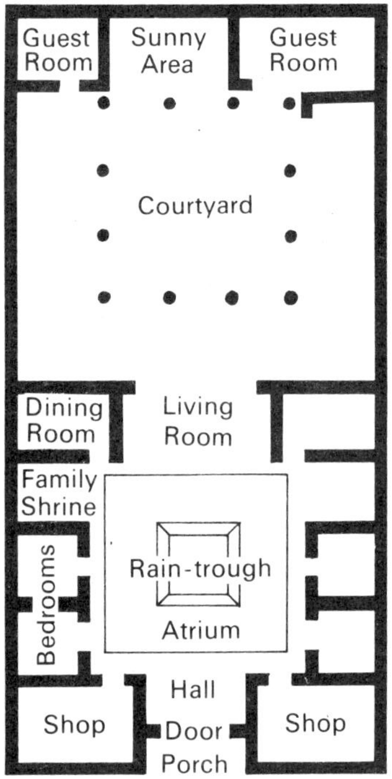


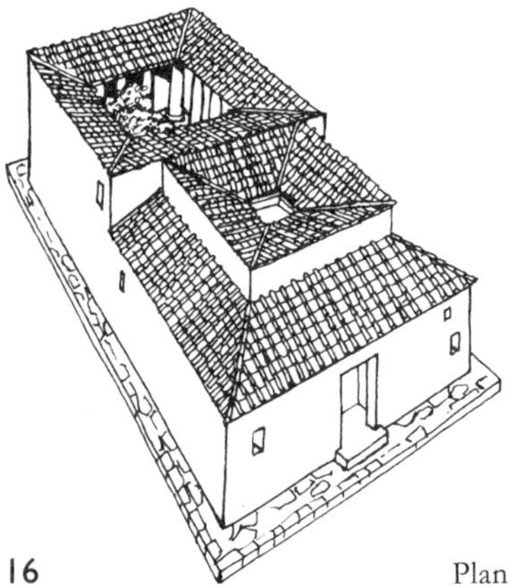

Plan of typical Roman town house

# Houses

The house of Valerius was not far from the centre of the town. From the outside there was little to see. One Roman description of a town house says,

> It turned a blind, unbroken wall to the street and all its doors and windows opened on its interior courtyards.

Inside the courtyard there was a beautiful garden with trees, flowers, statues and fountains.

*Look at the diagram of the town house of Valerius.*

1. *What is on either side of the front entrance of the house?*
2. *Is there another entrance to the house?*
3. *Roofs were tiled or thatched. There was an opening in the centre of the roof. Why? When might this be inconvenient? Suggest what might then be done.*

Inside, the house was large and comfortable although there was much less furniture than we have in our houses today. The picture (page 17, top) shows what the living room may have looked like.

The floor is made from small pieces of coloured brick or stone arranged in a pattern set in plaster or cement. This is called a *mosaic* floor.

1. *What items of furniture shown here might be used in a house today?*
2. *Artists decorated the walls with pictures painted on wet plaster. Why do you think this is not very often done today?*
3. *The window has small panes of greenish coloured glass. Suggest why there is not one large window pane.*
4. *What type of modern floor covering is rather similar in design to mosaic?*

When Valerius wished to entertain his friends or important people in Silchester he would give a feast.

Poor people ate the same kind of dull food every day, especially a kind of porridge made from wheat, but much of the food eaten was similar to what we eat today.

As a special treat, however, you might have cared for fried snails fattened in milk, mice cooked in honey or stuffed dormice!

1. *The Romans used honey as a sweetener. Can you guess what substance, which we use every*

*day as a sweetener, the poet Pliny was describing here?*

A kind of honey which collects in reeds, white like gum. . . . It is only used in medicine.

2. *Unscramble these letters to find some of the fruits and vegetables used in Roman Britain.*

SEAP RAPSPINS

PASPEL SARPRBERY

SNIPTUR MULSP ARPES

BBACASEG LECREY

The dining room of Valerius had no chairs. The diners ate lying on couches and resting on one elbow. Everyone ate with their fingers and washed their hands between courses. Slaves served the meal on a low table. Each couch could seat three people. Usually Valerius tried to provide suitable entertainment. Sometimes he would invite a poet to read some of his own poetry or have musicians to play background music. For a really special feast he might employ dancers too.

*Above:* Model of a Roman living room from Reading Museum;
*Below:* Romans at table (artist's reconstruction by Alan Sorrell)

## Shops

Ordinary shopkeepers and tradesmen in Silchester lived behind the shop where they worked. Some shopkeepers were freed slaves.

Many of the shops were in the forum or market place shown in the picture on page 15. Here people met to talk and to buy what they needed.

Antonia, the wife of Valerius, sent her slaves every day to do the household shopping. Only rarely did she go shopping herself for clothes and expensive things.

The shops in the forum had no windows, only an opening in the wall. At night the shopkeeper put up shutters to close his shop.

The pictures show stone carvings of Roman shops.

*1. What is sold in these shops?*
*2. How would these goods be displayed for sale in shops today?*
*3. Suggest some other kinds of shops or stalls you would expect to find in this town.*

# The Baths

Valerius and his friends went to the public baths nearly every afternoon. The baths were good places to meet friends and hear the latest gossip.

Antonia usually went to the baths in the morning when men were not allowed in.

From the plan of a Roman bath you will see that Roman baths were more like Turkish baths than swimming baths. They had a number of rooms at different temperatures. The heat came from a fire under the floors which were raised up on pillars. Slaves stoked the fire with wood. The visitor could sit at the side of the pool or take a plunge in the hot or cold water.

The grandest (Roman) baths in Britain were at Aqua Sulis which we now call Bath. The water here came from a hot spring and people believed it helped to cure rheumatism and skin complaints.

Like us, the Romans had central heating.

1. *Why would the Roman system of central heating not work today?*

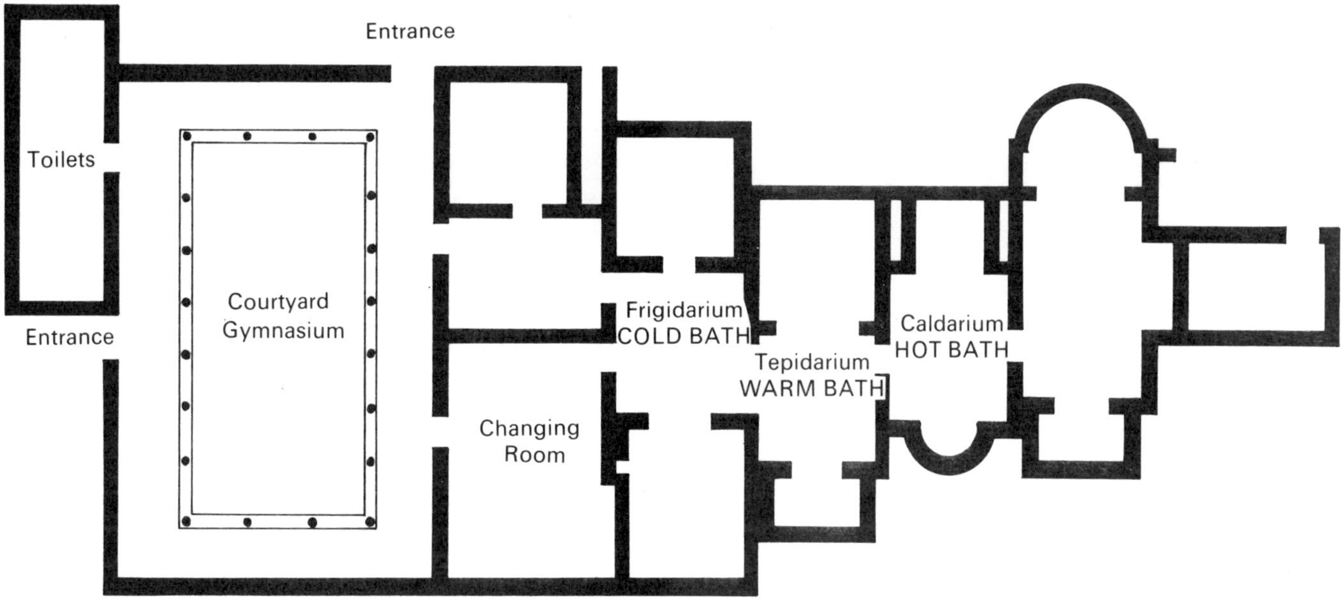

Here is a description of a bath by the Roman writer, Seneca.

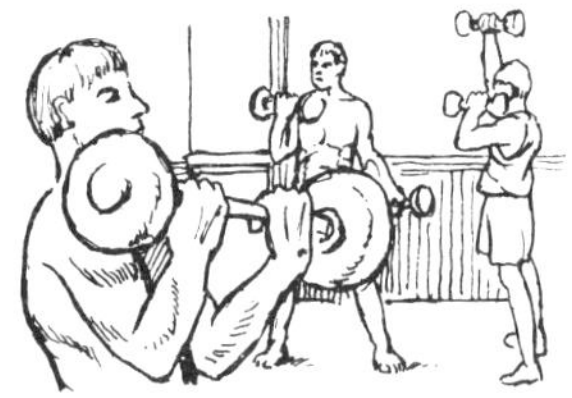

My house is right over a public bath. Every kind of human voice you can imagine rings in my ears. I hear groans, grunts, wheezing and panting, when athletes strain themselves while exercising with weights, or pretend to do so.

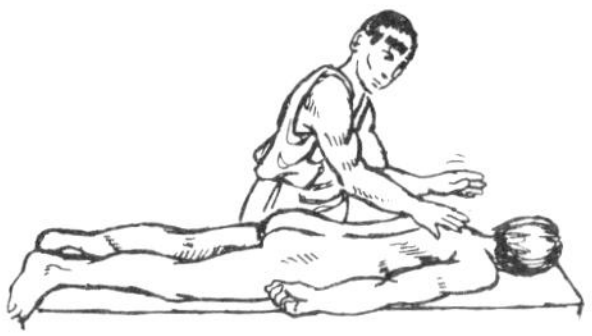

If there is a lazy person who is not exercising, but just having a massage, I can hear the sound of the smack of the hand slapping against his shoulders.

In addition there is the loud talker, the thief who has been caught in the very act of stealing and the man who loves to hear his own voice in the bath. Also there are people who make a great splash as they jump into the plunge bath.

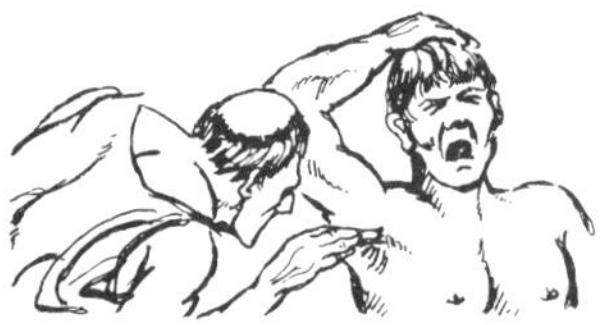

Another noise is made by the hair-plucker who constantly screams loudly to advertise his services. He is never quiet unless he is plucking someone's armpits and then I hear his victim scream with pain instead.

Add to that all the different cries of the sellers of cakes and sausages, the bakers and the food suppliers as they try to sell their wares.

1. *(a) Where did Seneca live?*
   *(b) Seneca complained of the noise. List some of the noises he could hear.*
   *(c) What could you have to eat at the baths?*
   *(d) Who made his victim howl?*
   *(e) Why might it be easy for a thief to steal?*



2. *Bathers could enter the various rooms in any order. Write the following down in the order you would prefer to do them.*

   *Exercise in the gymnasium*
   *Sweating in the hot room and hot bath*
   *Massage with scented oil before dressing*
   *Plunge in a cold bath to close the pores of the skin*
   *The warm room after undressing*
   *Scraping with a metal tool to remove dirt from sweating skin*

## Roman Britons

The Roman writer, Tacitus, explains why some Britons like Valerius wished to settle in towns.

The Roman governor Agricola gave encouragement and official help to the building of temples, public squares and private mansions. He educated the sons of the chiefs and said he would rather have a trained British person to work for him than skilled people from Gaul. Therefore instead of disliking the Latin language the Britons became eager to speak it well.

Important Romans always wore a toga on special occasions.

Tacitus explains,

our national dress came into favour and the toga was everywhere to be seen!

1. *What kind of help might Agricola give?*
2. *Why did Agricola choose Britons to work for him?*
3. *Which British people did he choose?*
4. *Was his plan successful?*
5. *Why did Britons learn Latin?*
6. *Why would the wealthy Britons wish to wear Roman dress?*

Many wealthy Britons who wished to follow the Roman fashion did not live in the towns. They built villas in the country. These villas were really large farmhouses with big estates round about. As well as the family house there would be stables, barns, a mill, housing for slaves and workshops for blacksmiths, carpenters and potters.

In the north and west of the country, however, the Britons went on living the same kind of life as before.

The villa farmers grew wheat. They reared herds of cattle and kept flocks of sheep. They sold their produce to the towns. The army relied on the villas for many of the things it needed.

1. *What were the things the army needed that could be supplied by the villas?*
2. *Some villas were centres of lead, tin or silver mining and iron smelting. What products might they provide?*
3. *Why would a villa owner be pleased to have his estate near a Roman road?*

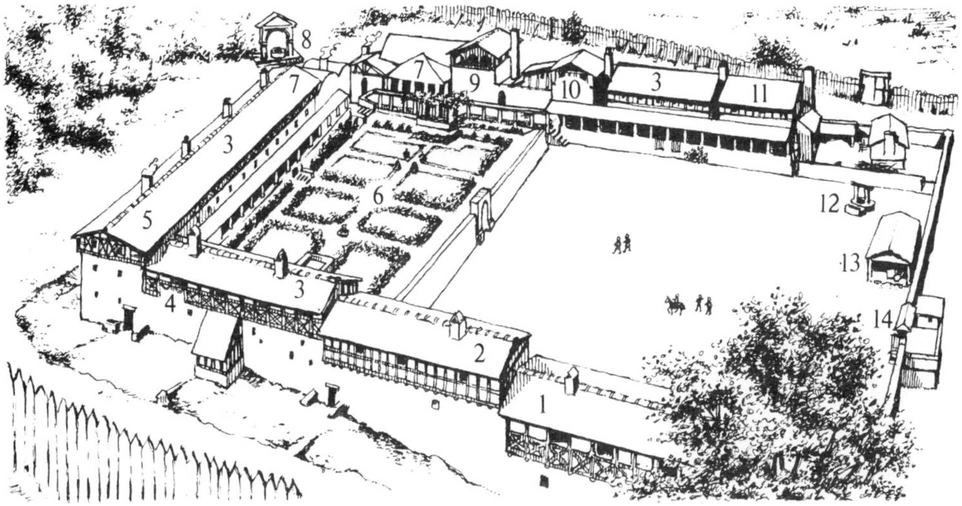


Drawing of reconstruction of Roman villa at Chedworth, Gloucestershire

1. Store
2. Servants' Quarters
3. Bedrooms
4. Kitchen
5. Dining Room
6. Atrium
7. Baths
8. Shrine
9. Hall
10. Furnace
11. Kitchen
12. Well
13. Barn
14. Main Gate

4. *Can you suggest why most villas were in the south-east of England? (Clue – crops, weather)*
5. *What type of labour made villa farming possible?*

If you want to find out more about Roman villas, there is interesting information in these books:

*Roman Britain* by Joan Liversidge, *Then and There* series (Longman)
*The Roman Occupation of Britain* by I. Doncaster (Longman)
*Lullingstone Roman Villa, Kent* (HMSO Official Guide)

# 5 Fighting for Rome

Roman Centurion
(Ermine Street Guard)

The year AD 150 was a special one for Gaius. His father Valerius was an official in Roman Britain who had once served under the great Emperor Hadrian. Now that Gaius was sixteen he, too, could join the army. Roman soldiers were still needed to keep the country in order and to defend it from the fierce tribes in the north and in Wales.

With other new recruits he had reported to the camp of the Twentieth Legion at Chester for training.

## Training and Discipline

The Roman soldier was very well-trained. A Roman writer, Vegetius, described the training of new recruits like Gaius.

Single stakes, six feet [about 2 metres] high, are fixed to the ground. The recruit attacks them as if they were an enemy, with a wickerwork shield and a wooden sword.

By continual practice they learn to march rapidly and in equal time. For an army that is split and disarranged by stragglers is always in serious danger from the enemy.

Another writer, Josephus, tells us that the Roman success was due to firm discipline and constant drill.

Every soldier is exercised every day as if it were in time of war. This is the reason they stand up so well in battle and do not tire.

For the first few weeks Gaius collapsed exhausted into bed each night. As well as marching and drilling, he had to practise hurling spears, fighting with a short sword, climbing walls and jumping ditches while wearing full armour. It seemed that he had no sooner fallen asleep than it was time to get up.

The trumpet was used to give signals and commands.

Their tunes for sleeping and watching and rising are given by the sound of trumpets,

says Josephus.

Gaius and his companions always rushed to obey the trumpet for punishment was severe. The penalty for desertion [running away from the army] was death. Other punishments were flogging, loss in pay or a cut in rations. A sentry who fell asleep on duty would be stoned to death by his comrades.

1. *What type of weapons were used in training? Would these be used in battle?*
2. *What similar type of training exercise might be carried out by a modern soldier?*
3. *Why was marching practice so important?*
4. *How would daily drilling and exercise help in battle?*
5. *Why would stoning to death be thought a just punishment for a sentry who fell asleep?*

## The Legion

Gaius had joined the Twentieth Legion. A Roman soldier was called a legionary. (Look back to page 10 to see how Gaius would dress.) Gaius was one of eight soldiers who shared a tent made of leather. They had a pack horse to carry it and other heavy equipment.

*1. How many men would be in a century?*
*2. How many troops were in a cohort?*
*3. What do you notice about the size of the first cohort in the diagram?*
*4. The 120 horsemen were not used as cavalry. What type of jobs might they be given? (Clue – messages)*
*5. Suggest why an older man was chosen as chief centurion.*

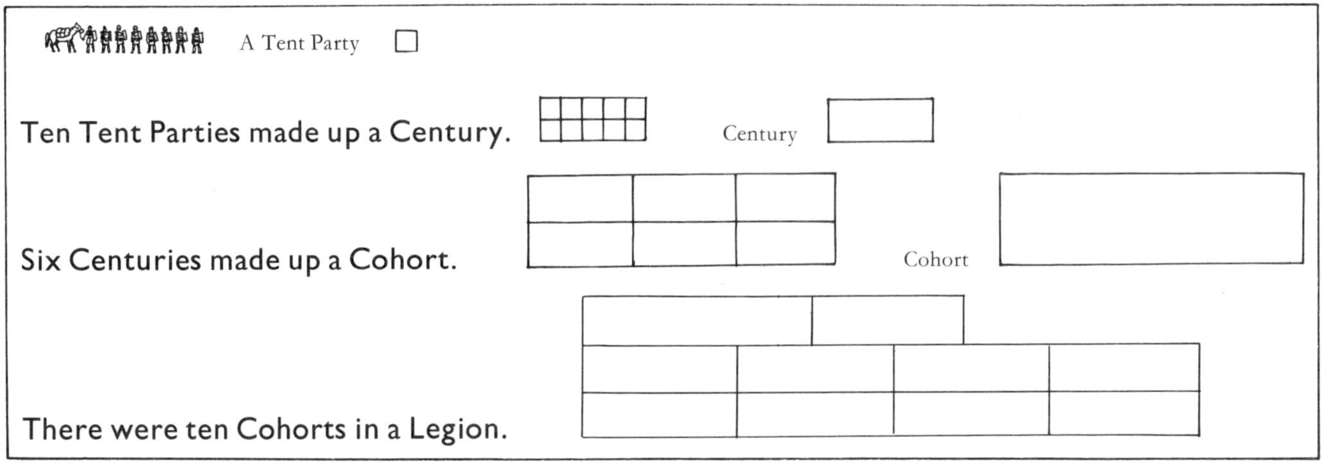


Although it had about the same number of fighting men, the first cohort also had tradesmen and all the clerks and officials who kept records, looked after the stores and helped in organisation.

The total number in a legion was about 6 000 men. There was a squadron of 120 horsemen.

The chief centurion in charge of the first cohort was a very important person. He was often quite old, nearly 60. He served for only one year and then retired on a large pension.

## The Standard

Gaius hoped that one day he might be chosen as a standard bearer. Each century had a standard, like the one shown in the picture, round which soldiers could gather in battle. The standards were pointed at the bottom like spears and had handles on the pole. The standard bearer wore a cover of animal skin over his helmet. He had to lead the soldiers into battle and must stand his ground so that other soldiers could see the standard and try

Standard bearer or signifer (Ermine Street Guard)

to get to it. The standard for the whole legion was a gold eagle. It was never taken from camp unless the whole legion set out.

The stone carving shows legionaries crossing a river on a bridge made of boats.

1. *How many standard bearers can you see in the picture?*
2. *How do you know that the whole legion is on this expedition?*
3. *Why would it be considered a disgrace to lose a standard?*

# Auxiliaries

The legionaries in the army were all Roman citizens like Gaius. This gave them special privileges. There were also auxiliaries who came from conquered tribes in different parts of the Roman Empire. Many auxiliaries had special skills. The best archers came from Syria and Arabia. Gaul and Spain produced good cavalry. Skilled slingers and stone throwers came from the Balearic Islands.

The auxiliaries had no armour over their leather jerkins. They got less pay, but when they left the army after 25 years they became Roman citizens and had money with which they could buy a farm and settle down and marry a local girl.

In a battle the auxiliaries fought in front. The legionaries followed. They hurled their deadly javelins before moving in close to fight with their short swords. Since it was more expensive to train and recruit a legionary than an auxiliary, commanders usually allowed the auxiliaries to face the first shock of an enemy attack. For example, Tacitus explains that when Agricola was organising his troops to fight against the Britons he arranged them with great care.

The auxiliary infantry, 8 000 in number, made a strong centre, while 3 000 auxiliary cavalry were thrown out on the flanks. The legions were stationed in front of the camp wall. Victory would be much more glorious if it cost no Roman blood.

An auxiliary cavalryman shown on a tombstone

*1. Why do you think auxiliaries joined the Roman army?*

*2. Give a reason why the auxiliaries fought in front in battle?*

*3. Draw a small diagram to show how you think Agricola arranged his troops. Why did he arrange them in this way?*

*4. Would you have preferred to be a legionary or an auxiliary in the Roman army? Say why.*

# Camps

Gaius had to learn how to dig ditches and set up walls of wooden stakes. Josephus tells us that when Romans moved into enemy territory

They do not begin to fight until they have made walls all round their camp. . . . If it happens that the ground is uneven, it is first levelled. Their camp is four-square and carpenters are ready, in great numbers, with their tools, to put up their buildings for them.

Another writer, Vegetius, says,

When the Roman army camps for the night it builds a defended city.

The camp was surrounded by a ditch and the earth was used to make a high wall. A fence of sharp stakes was put on top.

Josephus explains,

They also put up four gates, one at every side, large enough for the entrance of beasts and wide enough for marching out quickly if needed.

Inside the camp the leather tents were set up in rows.

They divide the camp into streets and place the tents of the commanders in the middle. In the midst of all is the general's own tent.

Roman forts and fortresses in Britain south of Hadrian's Wall. The three main forts are named

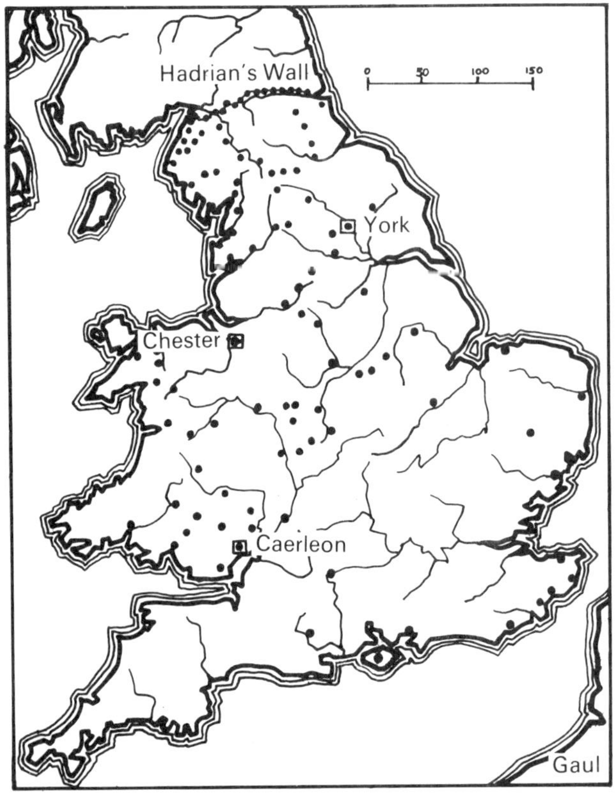


Plan of Roman marching camp or fort at Fendoch

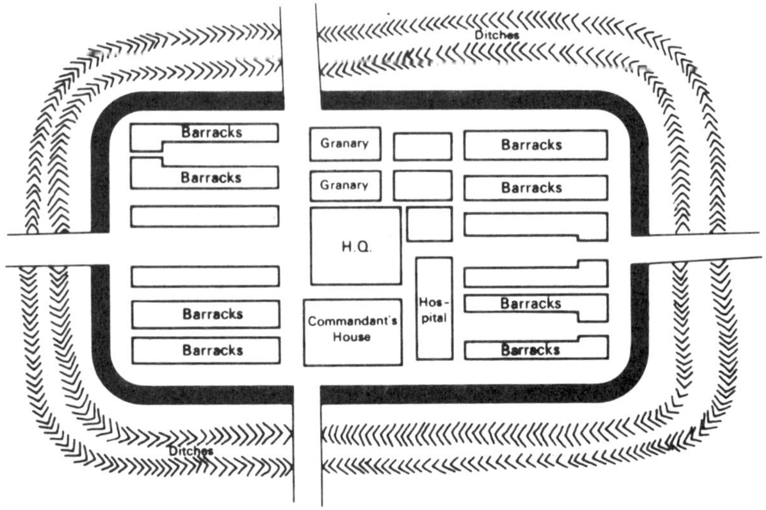

1. *What shape was a Roman camp?*
2. *Why would they level the ground?*
3. *How was the camp defended? Do you think 'a defended city' was a good description of a Roman camp? Say why.*
4. *A visitor to a Roman camp would always know where to look for the commander. Why?*

## Forts

If the Romans expected to stay for some time in one place they built a fort of stone.

Forts were built to guard fords or bridges, harbours for ships, crossroads and passes through the hills. Many forts were on the frontier. The plan for forts was the same all over the Roman Empire.
The picture shows a model of the large Roman fort at Chester which was once the home of the Twentieth Legion to which Gaius belonged. About 5 000 legionaries lived there. You will notice the high wall round the fort with a gate in each side. A wide road ran right through the fort with the headquarters

building at the centre. In the courtyard in front the guard was mounted [set up] and the centurions came to receive their orders. The statue of the Emperor and the regimental standards would be in the hall opposite.

Some of the long, narrow buildings were barracks where soldiers lived. Others were granaries which held a year's supply of grain.

Drill exercises and displays sometimes took place in the oval amphitheatre, outside the walls. Usually baths were built outside the walls also. Many baths had an altar to Fortuna, the goddess of Good Luck. Perhaps the soldiers played gambling games there.

Small villages often grew up round the fort where the soldiers' families and other people might live.

Some forts had auxiliaries stationed in them. At Bar Hill, an important fort on the northern frontier, there were auxiliaries from Germany and Syria. Some British auxiliaries fought in continental Europe near the Rhine and the Danube.

1. *What type of entertainment might be provided at the amphitheatre?*
2. *Why might people wish to settle near a fort?*
3. *Why were the auxiliaries not stationed in forts in their home areas?*

If you would like to find out more about the Roman army in Britain you might look at *Roman Britain* by Joan Liversidge, *Then and There* (Longman) or *The Romans in Scotland* by Oliver Thomson, *Then and There* (Longman).

Roman dice boxes and dice found near Hadrian's Wall

# 6 Life with the Romans ~ building and travelling

Roman soldiers often acted as builders. Many of them were skilled craftsmen.

1. *Write down three different jobs which the soldiers shown in the picture of a stone carving are doing.*
2. *Suggest two types of buildings on which soldiers might work.*
3. *To help them in the conquest of Britain, the Romans built good roads linking the main towns and forts. How would this help the movement of troops and supplies?*

## Roads

Roman roads linked all the parts of the Empire together. As trade developed in Roman Britain merchants, travellers and messengers with important government orders all used the roads.

Some Roman soldiers were surveyors who planned the line of a new road. To help them build straight roads they lit fires on the hilltops and sighted on the smoke. Where there were valleys, they made the roads follow the crests of the hills. The soldiers cleared away trees and bushes from the roadside so that there was no danger of a surprise attack. The roads stood higher than

Roman soldiers at work, from Trajan's Column

Model of a Roman bridge

Cross-section of a Roman road

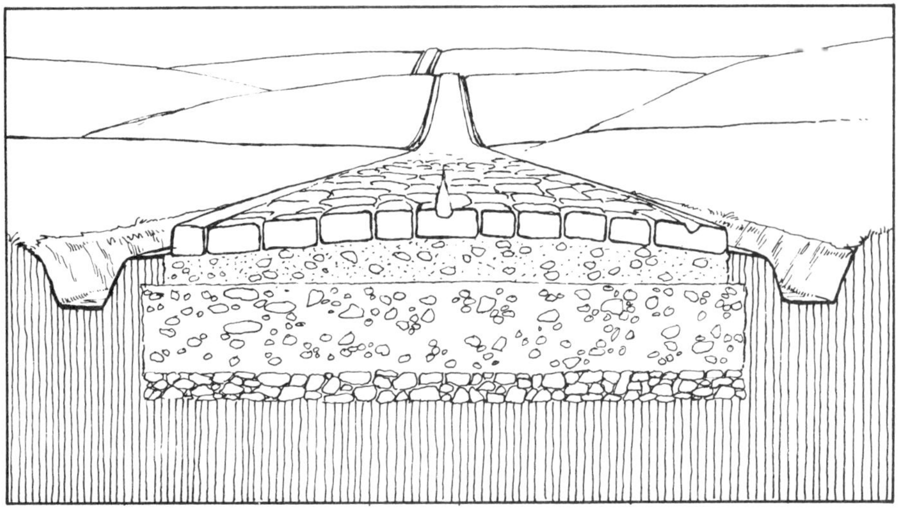

the ground round about and on each side were ditches to allow the rain to drain away. Before they put up a milestone, they paced out the distance between points on the road. Where there was no suitable ford to cross the river, they built a bridge.

When the surveyors had finished the soldiers usually forced local people to help them build the road. The map on page 31 shows the most important roads built by the Romans in Britain.

*1. Do you think road work would be popular? Say why.*

*2. (a) What was the surface of a Roman road made of?*

*(b) A great deal of wheeled traffic passed along a Roman road. Would the wagon wheels sink into the mud on a wet day? Say why.*

*(c) How did the Romans make sure water did not lie on the roads?*

People could walk along the roads or travel more quickly in light chariots. Messengers on horseback could travel as far as a 100 miles [160 kilometres] a day.

Very important places on a Roman road were the inns, where travellers could buy refreshments and change horses.

There were also rest stations along the Roman roads, a day's chariot journey apart. Here the traveller could get food, water for washing himself and a bed for the night.

Special rooms were set aside for people working for the government who might be travelling on important business or carrying letters and orders. There was stabling for horses and sheds for carts and carriages.

Unfortunately, after the Romans left Britain in the 5th century AD these fine roads fell into disrepair. It was over 1 000 years before such good roads were built again in Britain.

## Walls

The fierce tribesmen whom the Romans called Picts lived in the north in what is now Scotland. From time to time they raided the richer, more settled Roman area, robbing and burning houses and farms and stealing cattle. When the Roman Emperor Hadrian visited Britain in AD 122, he ordered a great stone wall to be built right across the country from the mouth of the River Tyne to the Solway Firth to separate the Romans from the people of the north.

Hadrian's wall is shown on the map. It was just over 73 miles long [117 km], and in places it was as high as 6 metres.

Later, in AD 142, a second wall, Antonine's wall, made of turf, was built even further north to mark the frontier, but it was abandoned after 50 years. The Romans found the mountainous country to the north of Antonine's wall more difficult to conquer. This was the Military Zone. Here we find remains of Roman camps, forts and walls.

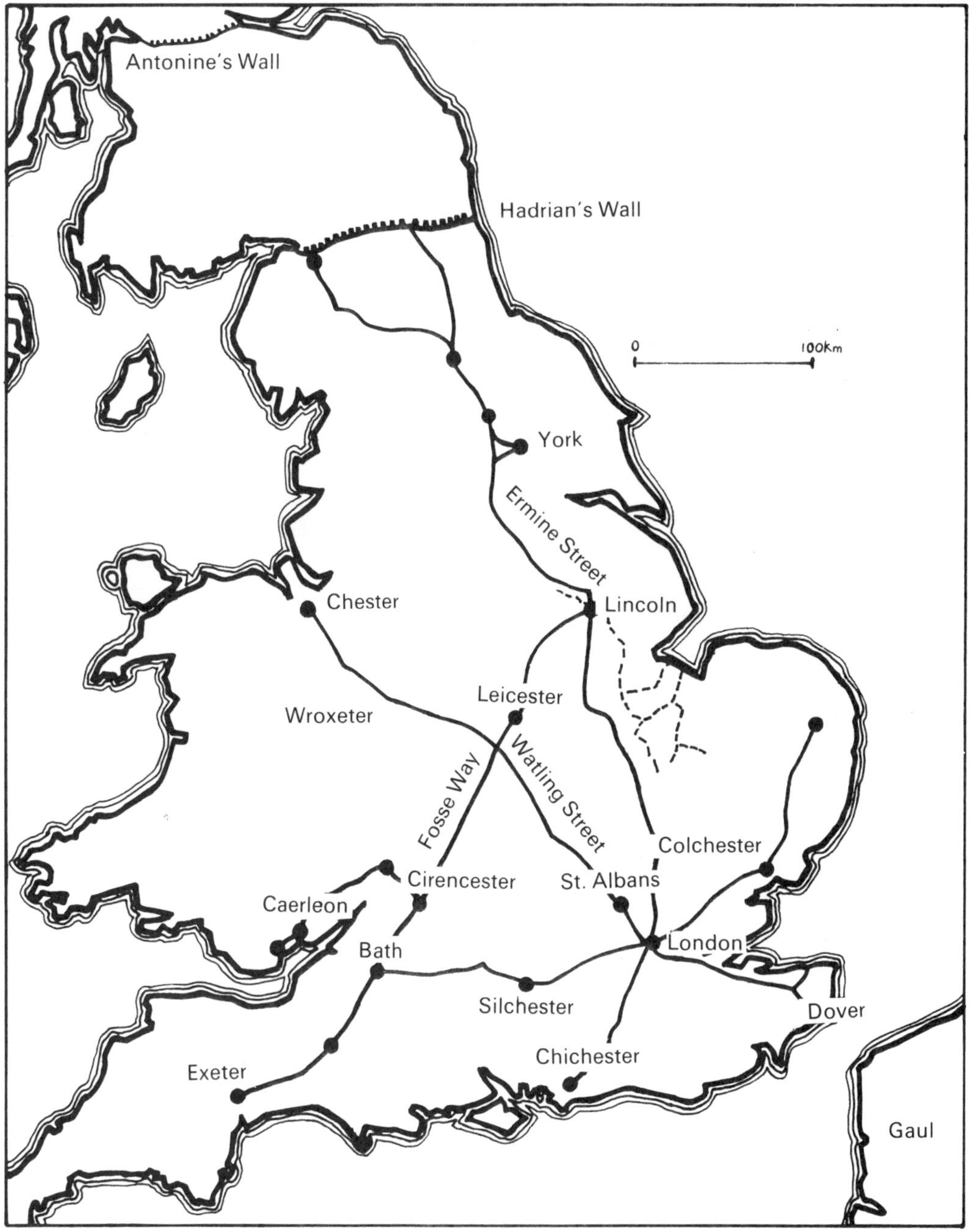

1. *Were the sites of the walls well chosen to mark the frontiers of Roman Britain? Say why.*
2. *Why would the wall be so high?*
3. *What different building materials were used for the walls?*
4. *Which wall would cost less to build and which would be stronger?*
5. *What Roman remains would you expect to find in the Civil Zone?*

The area to the north of Hadrian's wall was cleared of trees and bushes. In front of the wall there was a deep ditch. There were 17 large forts for the main garrisons. Every mile [slightly more than $1\frac{1}{2}$ kilometres] along the wall there was a small fort called a milecastle where up to 50 men could stay, and between each pair of milecastles were two turrets or signal towers. Behind the wall was a road called the Military Way.

Model of a mile castle on Hadrian's Wall

Model of Roman turret on Hadrian's Wall

The picture below is of the wall as it is today. It would not be very pleasant here in bad weather.

This poem by a modern poet is called 'Roman Wall Blues'.

Over the heather the wet wind blows,
I've lice in my tunic and a cold in my nose.

The rain comes pattering out of the sky,
I'm a wall soldier, I don't know why.

The mist creeps over the hard grey stone,
My girl's in Tungria, I sleep alone. . . .

She gave me a ring but I gambled it away,
I want my girl and I want my pay. . . .

1. *From the list below choose the words which best describe the soldier in the poem.*

| | |
|---|---|
| *discontented* | *warm* |
| *happy* | *bored* |
| *homesick* | *excited* |
| *uncomfortable* | |

2. *What do you think the soldier most dislikes about wall duty?*
3. *What other complaints does he have? (Clue – gambling, money)*

(You might like to read *Puck of Pook's Hill* by Rudyard Kipling, a story of Hadrian's wall in the 4th century AD.)

Hadrian's Wall today

# 7 A Roman Family

It is the year AD 320. Cornelius and his sister Marcia live in the south of Britain. Their father Lucius is a rich farmer. Long before, the family of Lucius had been important British warriors who had fought against the Romans. When they accepted Roman rule, they were given back some of their lands and allowed to farm. Although he was from Britain, Lucius was proud to be a Roman citizen. The descendants of British chiefs had become like the Romans in the way they lived and spoke, but ordinary country people still spoke the old language of the Britons.

1. *What kind of house will Cornelius and Marcia live in?*
2. *How would the Romans expect farmers like Lucius to help to pay for the government of the country? (Look back to page 21.)*
3. *What language would Lucius and his family speak?*
4. *What benefits would a rich farmer like Lucius see in Roman rule? (Clues – peace, travel, trade)*

## Schools

The stone carving in the picture shows a teacher and his pupils.

Cornelius did not go to school. Only the big towns had schools. He was taught at home by a tutor called Ballio.

The son of a rich man would be taken to school by a special slave called a paedagogus. He carried the boy's books and equipment and instructed him as he went along. He would report to the boy's father about his conduct at school.

Roman books were not like ours. They were written by hand on a long roll of parchment which was gradually unrolled with one hand and rolled up with the other.

1. *Which figure in the carving is the teacher?*
2. *Which figure might be the paedagogus. Why do you think so?*
3. *There are several books in the carving. Why would it take a long time to produce a book?*

# Lessons

When Cornelius first began lessons at the age of seven he learnt reading, writing and arithmetic.

Arithmetic was probably more difficult for Roman children for they used Roman numerals. To help them count more easily the Romans used a counting frame called an abacus.

Cornelius wrote on wooden tablets coated with wax with a *stilus* which was pointed at one end. The rounded end was useful for correcting mistakes.

As he grew older Cornelius learned to write with a reed or a bronze pen, like the one in the picture, on rolls of paper called papyrus.

Barrio the tutor was very strict. Cornelius started work soon after dawn and worked until late afternoon with only a break for lunch.

In the schools floggings were common. Pupils learnt some astronomy, history and music but most time was spent studying Latin and Greek writings and learning long poems by heart. Boys who hoped to have an important post when they grew up were taught the art of public speaking.

Tacitus said,

The man who wants to be a true citizen, able to deal with all matters of public or private

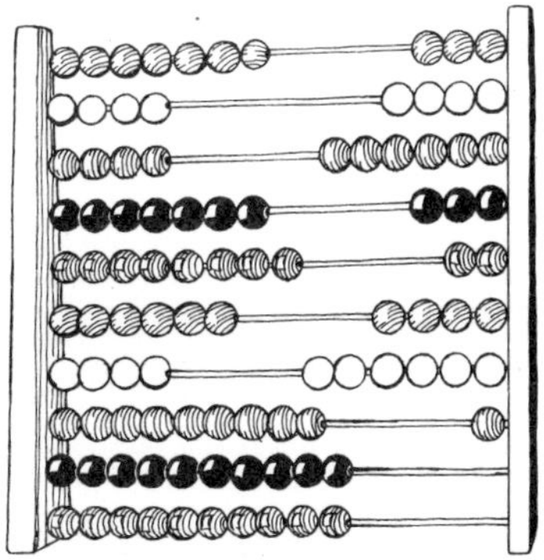

Abacus

Roman writing materials: remains of wooden board (tablet), ink pot with bronze pen, stilus

importance, able to guide cities with good advice and strengthen them with good laws or correct their mistakes with wise judgements – such a man must also be a good orator.

*1. What subjects were considered most important at school?*

*2. What sort of people did Tacitus think had to be good public speakers to be successful? Why do you think he believed this and do you agree about this for today?*

Cornelius was pleased when his tutor permitted him to practise wrestling or

Roman woman attended by her slaves

hunting. He loved to listen to his father's friends talk of chariot racing in the towns, and longed to be old enough to drive a swift chariot himself.

## Roman Girls

Roman girls were trained to become good wives. When they grew up they would take no part in government and have few rights under the law. Marcia learned how to read, write and count. Her mother taught her how to sew, spin and weave and how to look after the household and supervise the work of the slaves.

Marcia and her mother spent a great deal of time having their slave girls dress their hair with strings of pearls and jewelled hair pins. They knew this was how fashionable ladies in Rome behaved.

Some writers disapproved of this.

> All this wasted panic in arranging your hair! Why can't you leave it alone? One minute you are building it up, the next letting it down. Some women spend all their time forcing their hair to curl, others making it straight.

*1. How many girls are attending the lady in the picture on page 36, and what are they doing?*
*2. What is the chair made of?*

## Toys

*1. The little model at the foot of the page is made of bronze. How do you think it might have been used?*
*2. The other picture shows the kind of toy Marcia might have played with. What is it made of?*

## Religion

The family of Lucius were Christians. A small room in the villa was set aside as a church. In earlier times Christians had been persecuted and put to death. For example, this letter was written by Pliny, governor of a Roman province, to the Emperor Trajan in AD 113:

Your majesty, it is my rule to report to you anything which worries me. As regards the treatment of Christians, I have several problems. Should young and old be punished in the same way? Should those who give up Christianity be shown mercy? Should being a Christian deserve punishment even if the person is guilty of no other crime?

This is what I have been doing.

First I ask them if they are Christians. I give them three chances and warn them that if they say they are Christian they will be severely punished. If they are Roman citizens I order them to be sent to Rome. I was sent a notebook with the names of some supposed Christians. The sender did not give his name. I questioned these people. Anyone who denied he was a Christian was allowed to go if he prayed to the gods and offered incense and wine to your statue. Some said they had been Christians, but had given it up. To find the truth about what happened at their meetings I had two slave girls tortured but it seemed to be just superstitious rubbish. I think this is important, for the superstition has spread like the plague not only in the cities, but in the villages and the countryside as well. What should I do?

1. *About which group of people is governor Pliny writing?*
2. *List three problems he mentions.*
3. *How often does he question the Christians?*
4. *What happens if a Christian is a Roman citizen?*
5. *What information was Pliny given about Christians?*
6. *Do you think this was reliable? Say why.*
7. *How did those named in the notebook prove they were not Christians?*
8. *Sometimes Christians were accused of plotting against the Emperor. Can you suggest why people might believe this?*
9. *How did Pliny try to find out the truth? Was this a good way? Say why.*
10. *Why did Pliny think it was important to deal with Christians?*
11. *The Emperor Constantine declared Christianity the official religion of the Roman Empire in AD 313. How would this affect the Christians?*

Once the family of Lucius travelled to Silchester to visit the church there.

Before the rule of Constantine, the Romans had worshipped many gods and emperors at home and in temples. Look back to page 11 to see the temple built to the Emperor Claudius at Colchester. Here is a list of some Roman Gods.

Jupiter – King of the gods
Juno – Goddess of the sky
Venus – Goddess of love
Vesta – Goddess of the hearth
Diana – Goddess of hunting
Janus – God of the door
Mars – God of war
Pluto – God of the underworld
Apollo – God of the sun
Mercury – Messenger of the gods
Neptune – God of the sea.

A Popular god with Roman soldiers and merchants in Britain was Mithras who fought against the forces of evil. No women were allowed to enter his temple. In 1953 a temple of Mithras was found on a bombed site in London.

This carving of Mithras can be seen in the Wallbrook Museum, London

Bronze model of Mars
from the British Museum

# 8 The Empire

Roman Britain was only a small part of the great Roman Empire, which was 3 000 miles long and 2 000 miles wide [about 5 000 by 3 000 kilometres]. A hundred million people lived in it.

At the time when Jesus Christ was born in Palestine, the ruler of the Roman Empire was Caesar Augustus. The Bible tell us (*Luke* 2 *v.* 1)

There went out a decree from Caesar Augustus that all the world should be taxed.

Mary and Joseph had to go to Bethlehem to pay their taxes to the Roman Empire.

The map on page 41 shows the Roman Empire at the time of Caesar Augustus. You will see that, as well as Palestine, the Romans controlled Asia Minor, Syria, Egypt and North Africa.

On the borders of the Empire there were fierce barbarian tribes. The Romans needed large armies to defend the frontiers. The territories conquered by Rome became Roman provinces. Each province was ruled by a governor.

1. *How had the Romans won their empire?*
2. *Why would it be difficult to govern such a large empire?*
3. *Use an atlas to help you write down some of the modern names of countries in Europe which were once part of the Roman empire. Beside each write the products of that country which went to Rome (e.g. France – wine, cloth, olive oil).*
4. *What name was given to the province of Britain?*
5. *What did the Romans call the north of Britain?*
6. *Were all the soldiers in their armies Romans?*
7. *Why might this be a possible danger?*
8. *How did the Romans try to defend the frontier in Britain?*

*Key to Roman Trade Map on opposite page*

1. Olive Oil
2. Fruit
3. Wine
4. Grain
5. Fruits
6. Timber
7. Hides and Leather
8. Sheep
9. Horses
10. Gold and Jewels
11. Silver
12. Glass
13. Pottery
14. Lead
15. Tin
16. Bronze Goods
17. Marble
18. Parchment
19. Cloth
20. Dye
21. Slaves
22. Salt

## Fall of Empire

### Rival Governors

During the 3rd century AD the great Roman empire began to grow weaker. In some of the provinces there were wars between Roman governors who wanted to be Emperor.

A writer called Zosimus tells us that in AD 383 there was trouble in Britain.

Maximus had been a fellow soldier of Theodosius in Britain. He was offended that Theodosius was Emperor and he was not. So he encouraged the soldiers to hate Theodosius. The soldiers were easily persuaded to revolt and proclaim Maximus Emperor.

Another writer, Gildas, tells us,

Maximus behaved like a tyrant. He took a large

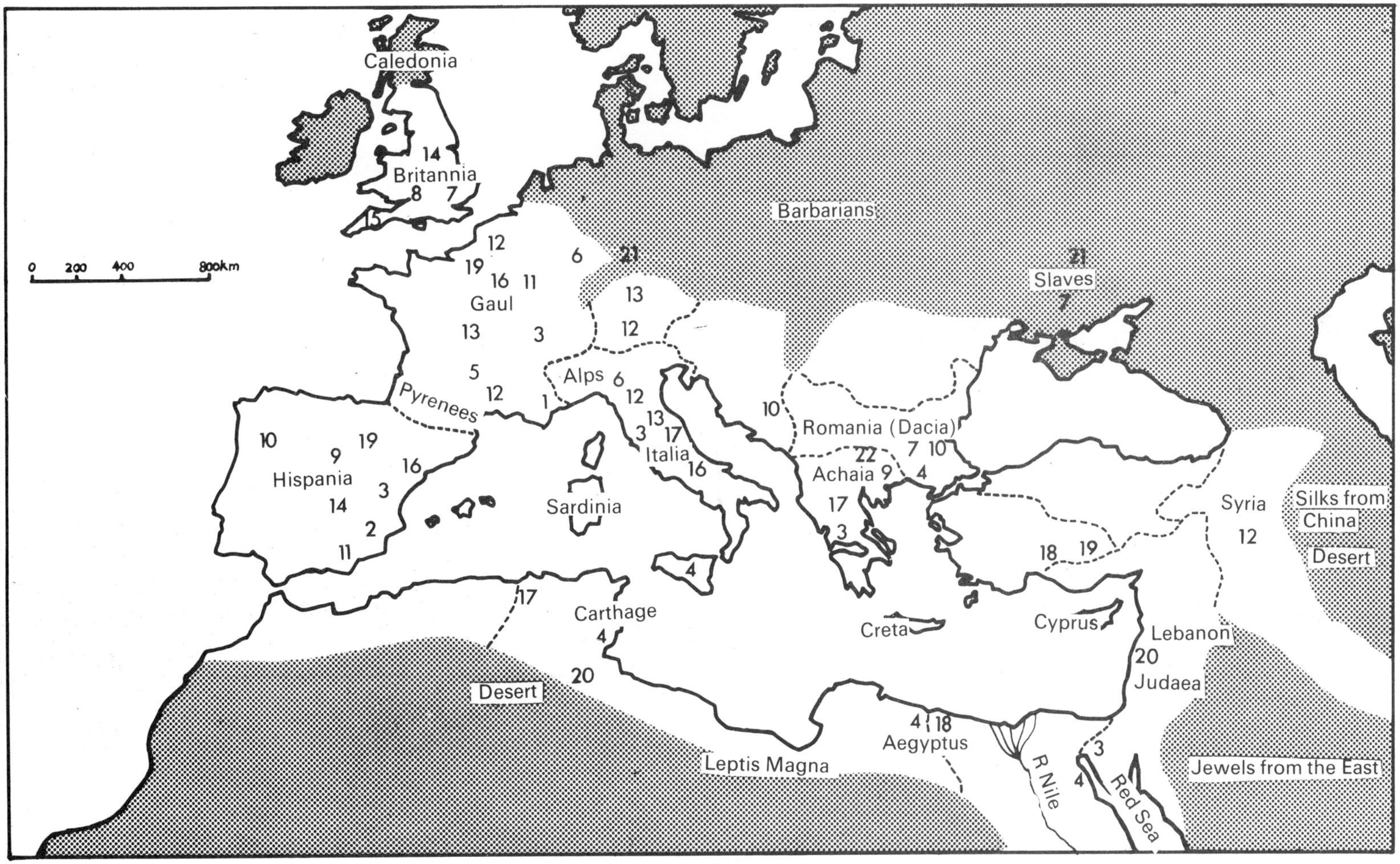


Trade in the Roman Empire (*key on page 40*)

number of traitorous soldiers across to Gaul. Now Britain was defenceless.

*1. Why would wars between emperors weaken the Empire?*

*2. Explain why Maximus organised a revolt.*

*3. Why do you think the soldiers in Britain supported him?*

*4. Why might the revolt of Maximus cause serious trouble for Roman Britain?*

## The Picts and the Scots

Gildas also tells us

Knowing nothing at all of the arts of war, Britain was crushed for years under the cruelty of two foreign nations – the Scots from the north-west and the Picts from the north.

1. *Pick out the phrase which shows the Britons were not used to fighting.*
2. *Had the Britons always known little about fighting? How had this happened?*
3. *Where did the Picts and the Scots come from?*
4. *Why did they choose this time to attack Roman Britain?*

## Appeal to Rome

Another writer, Nennius, tell us that,

Although the Britons had killed three Roman deputies they begged for Roman help when they were attacked by the barbarians.

Gildas explains,

They sent ambassadors to Rome with letters begging for an armed force to be sent to protect them. They offered loyal service to Rome if only the invaders could be thrown out.
Their rebellion was forgiven and a well armed legion was sent at once. When the Roman soldiers landed in Britain they went straight into battle. They killed large numbers of the enemy, who were all driven back beyond the frontiers, and the humiliated natives of Britain were rescued.

1. *How had the Britons rebelled against the Romans?*
2. *Why were the Britons now so anxious to have Roman troops sent to Britain?*
3. *What promise did they make to Rome?*
4. *Why do you think the Romans forgave their rebellions?*
5. *What action was taken? How effective was it?*

## The Saxons

All over the Empire barbarian tribes took the advantage of any weakness and plundered and raided across the frontiers. The greatest danger to Britain came from the Saxons. These fierce warriors came from north-west Germany to raid the British coasts. To deal with these raiders the Romans built special forts and signal towers along the east coast, near to rivers or harbours. A fleet was organised to patrol the coast. Swift horsemen were stationed near the forts.

1. *The man in charge of defending the coast was called the Count of the Saxon Shore. Why was this a good name for him?*
2. *A fort like the one in the picture on page 43 was not large. Why might it be better to have several small forts than one large one?*
3. *Why does the fort have a high tower?*

4. *What sort of signals would be given if the men in the fort saw Saxon ships approaching?*
5. *Why were these forts built near rivers or harbours?*
6. *This must have been an anxious time for people living in Roman Britain. If the Saxons landed what would they be likely to do?*
7. *If you were a Roman or a wealthy Briton with many rich and beautiful possessions, such as those illustrated on page 47, how might you try to protect them?*

## The Romans Leave

Eventually, in AD 410, the barbarian attacks on the Empire became so severe that the city of Rome itself was threatened.

Zosimus tells us that,

The Emperor Honorius sent letters to the cities of Britain telling them to look after their own security themselves.

1. *Why would it no longer be possible for Roman troops to protect Britain?*

A later diary (*The Anglo-Saxon Chronicle*) tells us that in AD 443

The Britons sent across the sea to Rome and begged for help but they got none because the Romans were engaged in a campaign against Attila, King of the Huns.

Soon afterwards the Vandals looted Rome. Many of the great buildings were in ruins. The people were starving. Everywhere there was confusion. Only in the eastern part of the Roman Empire around Constantinople did the civilised way of life of the Empire live on.

Reconstruction of Roman fort or signal station. Only the foundations of the original building are now visible on Castle Hill, Scarborough

# 9 Looking at the Evidence

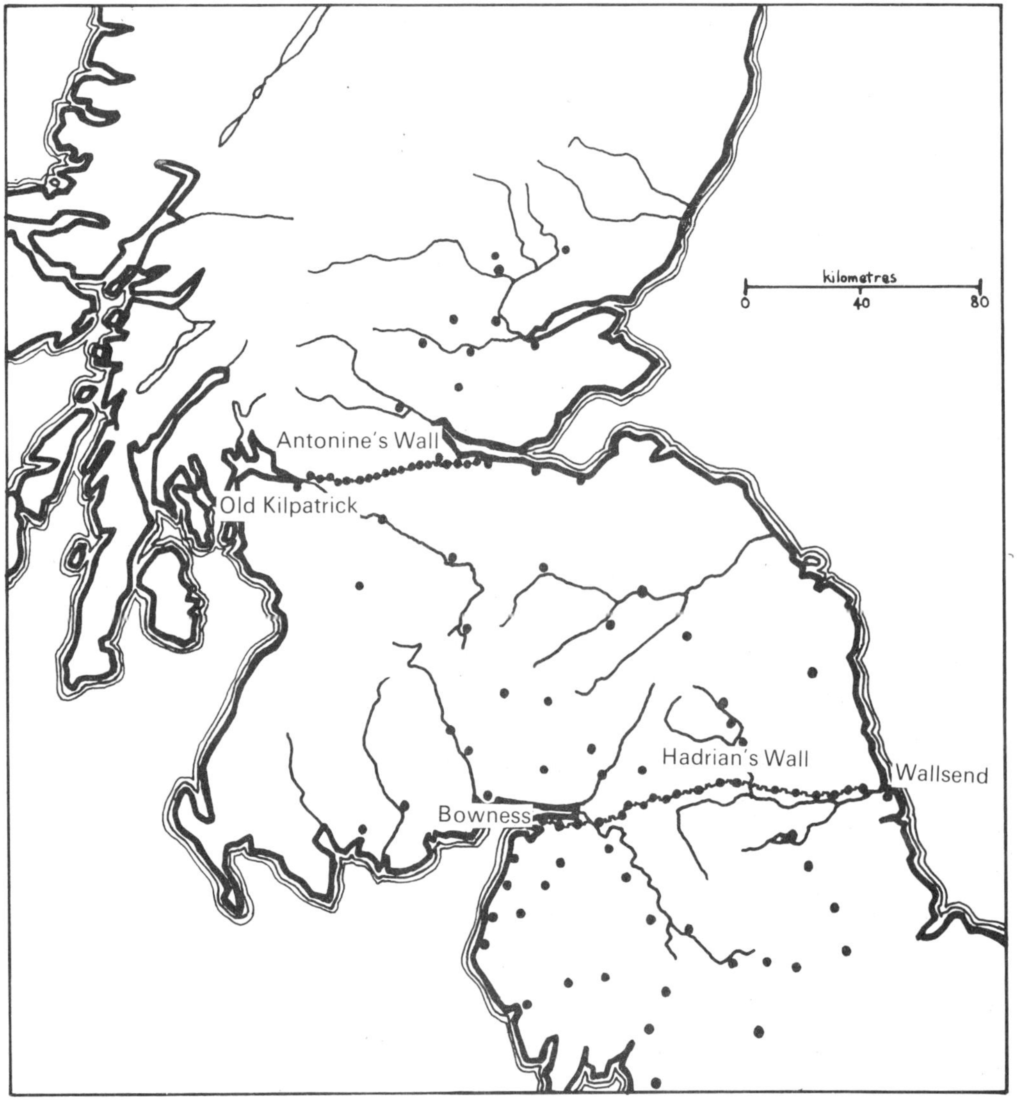


Roman forts and fortresses in Scotland

There are no Romans alive today who can tell us what life was like in Roman Britain. To find out we have to look at *evidence* or clues. Just as a detective examines clues to build up a picture of what happened when a crime was committed, a historian examines evidence to find out what happened in the past. One type of evidence is written evidence.

Look back to the introduction and Caesar's description of the Roman landing in 55 BC. Supposing a Briton had been describing the landing of Caesar and his troops, would he have said the same thing? Probably not. Caesar gives the Roman point of view.

Written evidence tells us a great deal about Agricola, a famous governor of Roman Britain from AD 78 to AD 85. His son-in-law, Tacitus, wrote a book about him in which he describes Agricola's work.

1. *How do you think Tacitus would know what Agricola had done in Britain?*
2. *Tacitus probably did not visit Britain himself. Do you think he would be a good source of information about Roman Britain in Agricola's time? Say why.*
3. *Tacitus describes how Agricola pushed into Caledonia (now Scotland) and built a number of forts. Can you think of any other evidence we could find to prove that the Romans built forts in Scotland? (Look at page 45.)*

This map shows the Roman forts in Scotland in Agricola's time. Tacitus tells us that in AD 84,

Agricola's troops advanced further north and built a number of marching camps like those described on page 26.

Another type of evidence helps us to know about these camps.

Photographs taken from the air at certain times of the year, in a certain light, show the outlines of forts like the one in the picture below, although there may not be any walls that we can see.

*1. How might an archaeologist discover further evidence after examining aerial photographs?*

Aerial view of Ardoch Fort, Perthshire

'The front line' from Trajan's Column

Tacitus tells us Agricola met the Caledonians at Mons Graupius, the Graupius Mountain. Over 30 000 Caledonians had united to fight the Romans. Tacitus describes one of their leaders, Calgacus, as saying

Most of these Roman troops have no country, or, if they have one, it is not Rome.

In the ranks of our very enemies we shall find hands to help us.

The battle of Mons Graupius was a fierce one. Agricola had cheered his troops by saying

These are the Britons with the longest legs – the only reason they have survived so long.

Tacitus admits that the Caledonians showed both courage and skill but the well-disciplined Romans won a great victory with few losses. 10 000 Caledonians were killed and Tacitus describes how

arms, bodies, severed limbs lay all around.

*1. Do you think Calgacus really spoke these words? How might Tacitus have found out?*
*2. Explain these remarks:*
*(a) Most of these Roman troops have no country (see page 25).*
*(b) In the ranks of our very enemies we shall find hands to help us.*
*3. How did Agricola try to encourage his troops?*

The battle was a great triumph for Agricola but we do not know exactly where it was fought. Tacitus does not give a clear description. It may have been near one of the forts between Fendoch in Perthshire and Stracathro in Angus. Some people think it was as far north as Inverness. Some day an archaeologist may find further evidence which will help us to find out where the battle took place.

*1. What might happen in the future to settle the argument?*

To find out more about Agricola and Mons Graupius you might like to look at *The Romans in Scotland* by Oliver Thomson, *Then and There* series.

The Mildenhall Treasure

# Bibliography and Sources

## Sources

Julius Caesar, *The Conquest of Gaul*
Suetonius, *The Twelve Caesars*
Dio Cassius, *Roman History*
Tacitus, *On Britain and Germany* and *Annals of Imperial Rome*
Vegetius, *Instituta rei militaris*
Josephus, *Wars of the Jews*
Pliny the Younger, *Letters, Book X*
Zosimus, *History*
Gildas, *On the Destruction of Britain*

## Further Reading

* A. R. Birley, *Hadrian's Wall*, HMSO, 1963.
S. C. Boyd, S. C. Phillips and I. M. Youds, *Roman and Saxon Britain*, Evans Brothers, 1969 (good for model building).
R. E. C. Burrell, *The Romans in Britain*, Pergamon Press, 1972.
P. Connolly, *The Roman Army*, Macdonald Educational, 1975.
I. Doncaster, *The Roman Occupation of Britain*, Longman Group, 1961.
A. Fox and A. Sorrell, *Roman Britain*, Lutterworth Press, 1961.
J. Liversidge, *Roman Britain* (*Then and There* series), Longman Group, 1965.
R. D. Lobban, *Roman Britain*, *(Quest Library)*, Oliver & Boyd, 1963.
R. J. Mitchell, *Roman Britain* (*Focus on History*), Longman Group, 1968.
M. & C. H. B. Quennell, *Everyday life in Roman and Anglo-Saxon Times*, Batsford, 1959.
* I. A. Richmond, *Roman Britain*, Pelican, 1970.
R. R. Sellman, *Roman Britain*, Methuen, 1964.
O. Thomson, *The Romans in Scotland* (*Then and There* series), Longman, 1968.
* G. Webster, *The Roman Army*, Grosvenor Museum Publications, 1956.

(* for the teacher)

## Exciting Stories

R. Sutcliff, *The Eagle of the Ninth*, Oxford University Press, 1970.
H. Treece, *Legions of the Eagle*, The Bodley Head, 1972.